101
Great Sauces

No Butter, No Cream, No Kidding!

John Ettinger

Prima Publishing
P.O. Box 1260BK
Rocklin, CA 95677

Production by Melanie Field, Bookman Productions
Copyediting by Marianne Rogoff
Illustrations by Richard Sheppard
Typography by Archetype Book Composition
Interior Design by Suzanne Montazer
Cover design by The Dunlavey Studio, Sacramento
Cover photography by Kent Lacin
Food styling by Èrez

Library of Congress Cataloging-in-Publication Data

Ettinger, John.
  101 great sauces—no butter, no cream, no kidding!: easy and delicious good-for-you sauces for every occasion/John Ettinger.
    p. cm.
  Includes index.
  ISBN 1-55958-498-X
  1. Sauces. I. Title II. Title: One hundred one great sauces—no butter, no cream, no kidding!
  TX819.A1E88 1994
  641.8′14—dc20
                                                  93-49715
                                                    CIP

94 95 96 97 98 RRD 10 9 8 7 6 5 4 3 2 1
Printed in the United States of America

How to Order
Single copies may be ordered from Prima Publishing, P.O. Box 1260BK, Rocklin, CA 95677; telephone (916) 632-7400. Quantity discounts are also available. On your letterhead, include information concerning the intended use of the books and the number of books you wish to purchase.

Contents

Mexican/South American

French

Indian/Oriental

Middle Eastern

American

Barbecues and Marinades

Desserts and Breakfast

Introduction

Sauces have suffered from a bit of an image problem. They are seen as agents of deceit, used only by bad cooks to disguise poorly prepared or overcooked entrees, or as harbingers of ill health with their rich creams and artery-choking butter.

I agree that some cooks seem to think sauces can save banquets. I have braved many versions of the Gravy-Like Barely Digestible Substance sauce recipe which I suspect all banquet cooks must share among themselves. It is in places where Velveeta is considered a dessert cheese that you will find sauces with the texture of motor oil and a little less flavor. What a shame, since saucing a food doesn't need to be a thick, buttery, caloric, or even particularly expensive, experience.

Changing an everyday plate of pasta, vegetables, or chicken into a one-of-a-kind dinner is easier than you might think, once you've discovered how to spin a little skein of stew stuff into something special with this wonderful bond that holds a good meal together.

Sauces are wonderful for matching accompaniments to ethnic entrees, great as appetizer dips to ready the family or friends for what is to come, and fine as finishing touches over a bowl of fresh fruit. They can make a holiday dinner more appealing by transforming meats or vegetables into something that is worthy of the event. Sauces can be quick too so the cook doesn't have to forego the gift-giving or egg-hunting to spend extra time in the kitchen.

I'm a Johnny-come-lately to my chef's cap. As a teen I ventured into the kitchen to ask when dinner would be ready, to make a sandwich or, against my wishes, to wash a dish. I only wandered into the kitchen to do some serious saucing after selling a weekly newspaper publishing business. I was in my mid-thirties and, after organizing the recipes I had collected over a decade, I began to spend my time dabbling, reading cookbooks, taking cooking classes and creating my own mistakes and masterpieces to the drip, drip, drip of Oregon skies.

Sauces, with their chameleon-like ability to turn a plateful of plain grains into something nourishing or even special, appealed to me most. They were fast, versatile and flavorful; all the things I liked best were components of sauces.

I began tinkering seriously with the sauces that would become this book two years ago. Since my younger son, Joseph, is allergic to dairy products, cooking without cream and butter became a natural way to do things. If I live to be 109 and a burden to him it will be his fault, his allergies hastened the end of the cream and butter sauces.

Many of the sauces in this book take less time to prepare than will the run to the grocery store for any missing ingredients. You will find a sauce for many kinds of ethnic foods, and for any vegetable dish you might dream up to complement an entree. If you detect a bit of a poultry prejudice you are right, we eat plenty of chicken. I encourage you to experiment with any of the sauces on foods other than the ones I've suggested.

A few notes on the recipes:

- If any olive oil will do, I simply specify olive oil in the recipe, but when a flavorful oil is needed I say extra-virgin.
- You should know that I am a pretty cool guy. That is, my hot sauces tend to be a little milder than other recipes you might try. If you like them on the hot side feel free to increase the appropriate spice or pepper.

- A salsa is an uncooked sauce. For example, I have included a black bean sauce and a black bean salsa and they have very different uses. Be creative—you may use salsas in any way you would use relishes or dips.
- Use care handling peppers. Serranos, pablanos, jalapeños and others can burn when you try to seed them. Be sure to wash your hands well after handling, or use gloves. I, and my eyes, speak from painful experience.
- A few of the recipes call for roasted peppers. To roast a pepper, first char it under a broiler, turning frequently, until blackened. Put it in a paper bag, close tightly, and let it steam itself for 20 minutes or so. The skin should come off quickly and easily. Jars of roasted peppers are also available in many grocery stores.
- Yogurt used in these recipes is plain, nonfat or lowfat as you prefer. The nutritional analysis is based on using nonfat yogurt.
- Low-salt chicken broth is recommended when using canned broth. If you use regular chicken broth, reduce or eliminate any salt called for in the recipe.
- Fresh herbs are always nice, if available. Some recipes will work only with fresh herbs and some work better with dried. Those are noted.
- For all recipes containing paprika use mild, not hot, paprika.
- Kosher salt is recommended for all my sauces. This salt has less bite than iodized salt.
- In recipes calling for chili powder use any commercial blend you prefer. Crushed red pepper is sometimes recognized as "pizza pepper," since it is frequently used in toppings for pizzas. It is also known as red pepper flakes.
- Throughout the book the preparation time includes cooking time. When standing, chilling, or marinating time is needed, it is indicated in parentheses.

Happy saucing!

1

Cucumber-Mint Sauce

Preparation time: 10 minutes

The cool, fresh flavor of this sauce makes it ideal for cold vegetables or with fish. Use fresh mint only and serve at room temperature.

1 cucumber, peeled, seeded, and chopped
Zest of 1 lemon
5 to 6 fresh mint leaves, coarsely chopped
Juice from $1/2$ lemon
$1/4$ teaspoon white pepper
$1/2$ teaspoon honey
$1/8$ to $1/4$ cup white vinegar
Scant $1/8$ teaspoon salt
$3/4$ cup peanut or walnut oil

Blend the cucumber, lemon zest, and mint in a processor until smooth. Add the lemon juice, pepper, honey, vinegar, and salt and blend briefly, then pour in the oil in a steady stream with the machine running.

Makes 2 1/2 cups

Each $1/4$ cup serving provides:

148	Calories	2 g	Carbohydrate
0 g	Protein	14 mg	Sodium
16 g	Fat	0 mg	Cholesterol

2

Cold, Creamy Lemon Sauce

Preparation time: 5 minutes (plus time to chill)

Pour this over fruit, such as orange wedges, or use as a
dipping sauce with fish. This has a very lemony taste and
is so flavorful you may be tempted to just drink it.

1/4 cup nonfat or lowfat yogurt
1/4 cup soft tofu chunks
1 teaspoon lemon juice
1 teaspoon lemon zest
1 tablespoon honey

Puree all in a blender. Chill.

Makes about 1/2 cup

Each 2 tablespoon serving provides:

35	Calories	6 g	Carbohydrate
2 g	Protein	12 mg	Sodium
1 g	Fat	0 mg	Cholesterol

3

Dill Sauce

Preparation time: 10 minutes

Fresh dill keeps longer than most herbs when tightly wrapped in the refrigerator; this sauce will last for a few days too. Use as a dipping sauce for crudités or cold fish. Or put a dollop on uncooked zucchini or cucumber for a refreshing addition to a summer barbecue.

2 tablespoons fresh dill, minced
1 cup nonfat or lowfat yogurt
1 teaspoon fresh lime or lemon juice
1 scallion, minced
$1/2$ teaspoon sugar
$1/8$ teaspoon salt
$1/8$ teaspoon white pepper

Combine all ingredients in a bowl and blend well.

Makes about 1 1/2 cups

Each 2 tablespoon serving provides:

12	Calories	2 g	Carbohydrate
1 g	Protein	28 mg	Sodium
0 g	Fat	0 mg	Cholesterol

4

Asparagus Vinaigrette

Preparation time: 10 minutes

Virtually all of the recipes in this book may be used for more than one food. Except this one. The taste of this vinaigrette is so seductive, it is the first thing I make when fresh asparagus becomes available.

½ cup olive oil
2 tablespoons Dijon mustard
¼ cup white wine vinegar
1 scallion, chopped
2 tablespoons fresh tarragon, minced
⅛ teaspoon salt
⅛ teaspoon pepper
1 pound asparagus, trimmed

In a small bowl, mix olive oil and mustard until thick. Mix in the vinegar, scallion, tarragon, salt, and pepper. Steam asparagus 3 to 4 minutes, until just tender. Rinse in cold water, drain, and place on a serving plate. Pour dressing over and serve.

Enough for 1 to 1½ pounds of asparagus

Each 2 tablespoon serving provides:			
142	Calories	4 g	Carbohydrate
2 g	Protein	134 mg	Sodium
14 g	Fat	0 mg	Cholesterol

5

Sesame-Ginger Sauce

Preparation time: 10 minutes

This works well as a dipping sauce, or poured over
cooked vegetables. It has a sweet and sour quality.

2 tablespoons fresh lemon juice
2 tablespoons fresh ginger, grated
1 tablespoon white wine vinegar
2 tablespoons sesame oil
1 tablespoon mustard
1 clove garlic, minced
1 teaspoon brown sugar
1 teaspoon honey
$^1/_3$ to $^1/_2$ cup vegetable oil

Place all ingredients except vegetable oil in a blender and
process until smooth. Slowly add oil until mixture thickens.

Makes about $^3/_4$ cup

Each 2 tablespoon serving provides:

161	Calories	3 g	Carbohydrate
0 g	Protein	33 mg	Sodium
17 g	Fat	0 mg	Cholesterol

6

Orange-Ginger Relish

Preparation time: 5 minutes

The orange and ginger flavors give this quick relish a brisk, tangy flavor. Try it with Indian dishes, pork, or poultry.

1 orange, peeled and chopped with juice
1 teaspoon fresh ginger, grated
1 teaspoon sugar
1 teaspoon Dijon mustard

Mix all ingredients together.

Makes about ³/₄ cup

Each 2 tablespoon serving provides:

15	Calories	3 g	Carbohydrate
0 g	Protein	23 mg	Sodium
0 g	Fat	0 mg	Cholesterol

7

Plum Chutney

Preparation time: 2 1/2 hours

My sister Virginia is the author of this delightful chutney.
She quadruples the recipe so she always has a jar in the
pantry. Use it with curries, roast turkey, or lamb.

2 cups plum pulp
1/2 cup white sugar
1/2 cup brown sugar
1/3 cup cider vinegar
1 teaspoon mustard seed
1/4 cup crystallized ginger, cut into thin strips
1 teaspoon salt
1 clove garlic, thinly sliced
1/4 cup golden raisins
1/4 cup red onion, thinly sliced
1 teaspoon crushed red pepper

Mix together sugars and vinegars and boil 10 minutes. Add
remaining ingredients and simmer 2 hours or until thickened.

Makes about 3 cups

Each 1/2 cup serving provides:

229	Calories	58 g	Carbohydrate
1 g	Protein	355 mg	Sodium
1 g	Fat	0 mg	Cholesterol

8

Apple Chutney

Preparation time: 50 minutes

Here is a chutney that goes well with many things, but especially with pork. You can also serve it alongside vegetables or with ham. Use Granny Smith or other tart apples.

3 cups apples, diced
1 cup cider vinegar
1 teaspoon cinnamon
$1/4$ teaspoon ground cloves
$1/2$ cup raisins
$1/2$ cup brown sugar
$1/4$ cup fresh ginger, minced
Juice from 1 lemon
$1/8$ teaspoon salt

Put all ingredients in a saucepan on low-medium heat and simmer about 45 minutes, or until apples are soft.

Makes about 3 1/2 cups

Each $1/4$ cup serving provides:

70	Calories	18 g	Carbohydrate
0 g	Protein	18 mg	Sodium
0 g	Fat	0 mg	Cholesterol

9

Cranberry Chutney

Preparation time: 30 minutes

Sure, this goes great with turkey, but try it with other poultry too. If you keep the lid on during the cooking and cooling, it increases the chance of keeping the cranberries whole.

1 bag fresh cranberries
³/₄ cup sugar
¹/₈ teaspoon baking powder
¹/₈ teaspoon salt
1¹/₂ cups water
¹/₄ cup raisins
¹/₂ cup orange zest

Place cranberries, sugar, baking powder, and salt in a kettle with ¹/₂ cup of water, stir, and heat. When near boiling, cover tightly and simmer 15 minutes. Remove from heat and let mixture cool completely with cover on. Stir raisins and orange zest into 1 cup of water and boil gently about 5 minutes. Carefully combine the cooled raisins with the orange zest with the cranberries.

Makes about 2 cups

Each ¹/₄ cup serving provides:

104	Calories	27 g	Carbohydrate
0 g	Protein	27 mg	Sodium
0 g	Fat	0 mg	Cholesterol

10

Dried Cherry Chutney

Preparation time: 15 minutes (plus 2 hours standing time)

This is delicious with grilled lamb but try it with other meats as well, including poultry.

2 cups dried cherries, rehydrated and chopped
2 shallots, minced
2 cloves garlic, minced
⅛ cup distilled white vinegar
1 tablespoon lemon juice
½ teaspoon cinnamon
1 tablespoon fresh ginger, grated
2 tablespoons sugar
1 cup dry red wine (Pinot Noir recommended)

Combine all ingredients in a saucepan and cook until the shallots and garlic are soft. Let stand 2 hours before serving, stirring occasionally.

Makes about 2 cups

Each ¼ cup serving provides:

159	Calories	35 g	Carbohydrate
2 g	Protein	3 mg	Sodium
2 g	Fat	0 mg	Cholesterol

11

Quick Tomato Sauce

Preparation time: 30 to 60 minutes

I must have spent a lot of time happily stirring a pot of tomato sauce in a previous life. Tomato sauce is my comfort food. When in the air over what to fix I make a tomato sauce, usually my Dependable Red, but occasionally without a recipe. Every cook should have a quick and easy tomato sauce, to pour over pasta, fish, meat, or vegetables. This is my version.

1 small onion, chopped
2 cloves garlic, minced
$^{1}/_{4}$ cup extra-virgin olive oil
3 tablespoons basil (or other fresh herb), chopped or
 1 tablespoon dried
1 tablespoon fresh oregano or 1 teaspoon dried
1 bay leaf
1 28-ounce can crushed tomatoes
$^{1}/_{4}$ teaspoon salt
$^{1}/_{4}$ teaspoon pepper

In a skillet or saucepan, sauté onion and garlic in olive oil for 3 to 4 minutes. Add the remaining ingredients and simmer at least 30 minutes, preferably 1 hour, stirring occasionally.

Makes about 3 cups

Each $^{1}/_{2}$ cup serving provides:

118	Calories	8 g	Carbohydrate
2 g	Protein	424 mg	Sodium
9 g	Fat	0 mg	Cholesterol

12

Red Pepper Sauce

Preparation time: 30 minutes

I'm all thumbs when it comes to peeling peppers so I
sometimes cop out and use the bottled ones, rather than
roasting my own. We eat this sauce with poultry, and it is
good on seafood. It also makes a great pizza sauce—just
add ¼ cup of fresh basil leaves about 5 minutes before it
is finished.

3 cups red bell peppers, seeded, cored, and roasted
1 16-ounce can tomatoes, drained
1 clove garlic, minced
1 scallion, minced
½ teaspoon fresh oregano, chopped or
    ¼ teaspoon dried
Pinch of cayenne
⅛ teaspoon salt
⅛ teaspoon pepper
⅓ cup extra-virgin olive oil
1 tablespoon red wine vinegar
¼ cup fresh basil (optional)

Place peppers, tomatoes, garlic, and scallion in a food
processor and blend until smooth. Add cayenne, salt, and
pepper and blend. Pour into a saucepan with the olive oil

and simmer for 15 to 20 minutes or until thickened, stirring occasionally. Stir in red wine vinegar, add fresh basil if desired, and serve.

Makes 4 cups

Each ½ cup serving provides:

107	Calories	7 g	Carbohydrate
1 g	Protein	128 mg	Sodium
9 g	Fat	0 mg	Cholesterol

13

Amatrician Sauce

Preparation time: 35 minutes

This pasta sauce, so named because it originated in the town of Amatrice, northeast of Rome, is often made with many other ingredients, including anchovies. This version closely follows the classic recipes.

2 tablespoons extra-virgin olive oil
1 onion, minced
1 cup pancetta, cut into small cubes
$^{1}/_{4}$ teaspoon crushed red pepper
1 28-ounce can tomatoes
$^{1}/_{8}$ teaspoon salt
$^{1}/_{8}$ teaspoon pepper

Sauté onion and pancetta for 10 minutes in the olive oil. Add remaining ingredients, chopping tomatoes in the pot, and simmer 20 minutes, stirring frequently.

Makes about 3 $^{1}/_{2}$ cups

Each $^{1}/_{2}$ cup serving provides:

131	Calories	7 g	Carbohydrate
6 g	Protein	675 mg	Sodium
9 g	Fat	0 mg	Cholesterol

14

Tomato-Basil Salsa

Preparation time: 10 minutes

This salsa or relish is good on beef, with sausage, or in sandwiches.

$^1\!/_2$ cup red bell pepper, diced
$^1\!/_4$ cup scallions, diced
$^1\!/_3$ cup white wine vinegar
2 to 3 Roma tomatoes, seeded and finely chopped
2 to 3 tablespoons fresh basil, torn into small pieces

Combine all ingredients in a bowl and stir.

Makes about 2 cups

Each $^1\!/_4$ cup serving provides:

7	Calories	2 g	Carbohydrate
0 g	Protein	2 mg	Sodium
0 g	Fat	0 mg	Cholesterol

15

Chick-pea Sauce

Preparation time: 45 to 90 minutes

I was in my twenties before I ever had garbanzos in anything except the vinegary Three Bean Salads sold in delis. Garbanzos, or chick-peas, are generally identified with Middle Eastern cooking, but this sauce is adapted from an Italian version.

1/2 cup olive oil
1 small onion, chopped
1 clove garlic, minced
3 tablespoons fresh basil, minced
1/4 cup tomato sauce
1/8 teaspoon salt
1/8 teaspoon pepper
2 16-ounce cans of chick-peas (garbanzos) or 2 cups
    dried, soaked in water overnight
1 cup water if needed

In a skillet, heat olive oil and sauté the onion until soft, about 5 minutes. Add garlic and basil, pour in tomato sauce, and season. Stir in the chick-peas and add water (fresh or from the can) to cover. Simmer until tender — about 90 minutes for dried peas and 30 minutes for canned. Puree half the sauce, then return to the skillet. Add water if needed for consistency.

Makes about 4 cups

Each ½ cup serving provides:

274	Calories	30 g	Carbohydrate
6 g	Protein	504 mg	Sodium
15 g	Fat	0 mg	Cholesterol

16

Romesco

Preparation time: 10 minutes

This sizzling Catalonian sauce is used to enliven seafood.
It works well with vegetables too. For a cooler version
use less hot pepper.

1 tomato, peeled, seeded, and chopped
½ red bell pepper, peeled, seeded, and chopped
1 tablespoon crushed red pepper
½ jalapeño or other hot pepper, coarsely chopped
2 cloves garlic, minced
2 tablespoons slivered almonds, toasted
1 cup olive oil
⅓ cup dry white wine
⅛ teaspoon salt
⅛ teaspoon pepper

Put all ingredients in a blender or processor and blend
until almost smooth, leaving some texture. Serve at
room temperature.

Makes about 3 cups

Each ½ cup serving provides:

346	Calories	2 g	Carbohydrate
1 g	Protein	43 mg	Sodium
37 g	Fat	0 mg	Cholesterol

17

Dependable Red

Preparation time: 1 1/2 hours

This delicious spaghetti sauce is simply Dependable Red
for us. Great with spaghetti and meatballs or sausage.
You can also cook other vegetables in the sauce, such as
sliced zucchini (add with the mushrooms) or sliced carrot
(sauté with the onion and garlic).

1/4 cup olive oil
2 onions, chopped
4 cloves garlic, minced
2 bell peppers, chopped
3/4 pound mushrooms, sliced thick
1 bay leaf
1 28-ounce can tomatoes with juice
2 tablespoons tomato paste
1 tablespoon sugar
1 tablespoon fresh rosemary or 1/2 teaspoon dried
1 tablespoon fresh oregano or 1/2 teaspoon dried
1 tablespoon fresh thyme or 1/2 teaspoon dried
5 to 6 tablespoons fresh basil, chopped or
    3 tablespoons dried
1/2 teaspoon garlic powder
1/8 teaspoon chili powder
1/8 teaspoon dill
1/4 teaspoon salt
1/4 teaspoon pepper

continued next page

Sauté onions, garlic, pepper, and mushrooms in olive oil over medium heat until onions are soft, about 5 minutes. Add remaining ingredients and simmer for an hour or so.

Makes 4+ cups

Each ½ cup serving provides:

124	Calories	14 g	Carbohydrate
2 g	Protein	254 mg	Sodium
7 g	Fat	0 mg	Cholesterol

18

Creamy Rosemary Sauce

Preparation time: 10 minutes

In Japan, rosemary's wonderful flavor is thought to enhance one's attitude or energy; rosemary is even put in office air filters to chase away afternoon lethargy. Try this sauce as a dressing on asparagus, or over a salad of walnuts, green apples, and pears.

1 tablespoon fresh rosemary, crushed
1 clove garlic, minced
1 teaspoon Dijon mustard
1 egg yolk
2 tablespoons red wine vinegar
6 tablespoons peanut or walnut oil

Crush rosemary in a bowl using the back of a spoon (or use a mortar and pestle), then stir in garlic and mustard. Whisk in the egg yolk, followed by the vinegar. Slowly add oil, whisking constantly.

Makes about ³/4 cup

Each tablespoon serving provides:

66	Calories	0 g	Carbohydrate
0 g	Protein	11 mg	Sodium
7 g	Fat	16 mg	Cholesterol

19

Tuscan Sauce

Preparation time: 55 minutes

This sauce has the sharp flavors found in Tuscan foods, and makes a hearty spaghetti sauce.

½ cup olive oil
2 cloves garlic, minced
1 small onion, minced
1 small eggplant, peeled and diced
10 mushrooms, quartered
1 Italian sausage, sweet or hot
1¼ cups red wine
1 28-ounce can tomatoes
2 tablespoons fresh basil, torn into small pieces

Heat olive oil in a saucepan and sauté garlic and onion until soft. Add eggplant and mushrooms. Remove sausage from its casing and add, breaking it up in the pan. Cook over medium-high heat, stirring frequently or even constantly, until sausage is lightly cooked, about 10 minutes. Add the red wine and simmer on medium-high heat for 10 minutes. Add tomatoes and their juice, reduce heat, and simmer for 15 minutes. Put in the basil and cook 10 minutes more, adding water or more wine if desired.

Makes about 4 cups

Each ½ cup serving provides:

197	Calories	9 g	Carbohydrate
3 g	Protein	245 mg	Sodium
16 g	Fat	7 mg	Cholesterol

20

Italian Fish Sauce

Preparation time: 10 minutes

This sauce, inspired by the many wonderful fish sauces of southern Italy, is good with baked fish.

$^1/_2$ cup parsley, finely minced
$^1/_3$ cup pine nuts, chopped
1 tablespoon capers, chopped
$^1/_4$ cup fine bread crumbs
1 clove garlic, minced
1 to 2 tablespoons white wine vinegar
4 to 5 Greek olives, pitted and minced

Mix all ingredients thoroughly. Serve over fish.

Makes about 1$^1/_2$ cups

Each $^1/_4$ cup serving provides:

73	Calories	5 g	Carbohydrate
3 g	Protein	128 mg	Sodium
6 g	Fat	0 mg	Cholesterol

21

Red Pepper-Basil Sauce

Preparation time: 15 minutes (plus 30 minutes standing time)

Cayenne complements the roasted pepper flavor in this sauce. Try it with fish, meat, or poultry.

2 red peppers, roasted, peeled, and chopped
1 teaspoon white wine vinegar
1/8 teaspoon salt
1/8 teaspoon cayenne
1/4 cup nonfat or lowfat yogurt
1/4 cup fresh basil, torn into small pieces

In a blender, puree red peppers with vinegar, salt, and cayenne. Remove to a bowl and whisk in the yogurt and basil. Let stand about 30 minutes.

Makes about 1 1/2 cups

Each 1/4 cup serving provides:

12	Calories	2 g	Carbohydrate
1 g	Protein	47 mg	Sodium
0 g	Fat	0 mg	Cholesterol

22

Tuna Sauce

Preparation time: 10 minutes

This is a most unusual pasta sauce, since most people aren't accustomed to eating tuna fish tossed with noodles. Try it with fettucine.

1 6½-ounce can tuna fish, packed in oil
Juice from 1 lemon
¼ cup walnuts, chopped
3 tablespoons fresh parsley, chopped
½ teaspoon soy sauce
1 tablespoon fresh basil, finely chopped
1 teaspoon fresh dill, finely chopped (optional)
⅓ to ½ cup extra-virgin olive oil
⅛ teaspoon salt
⅛ teaspoon pepper

Drain tuna and place in a blender or processor. Add the rest of ingredients except the olive oil, salt, and pepper and puree. Add olive oil a little at a time, pulsing to blend. Stir in salt and pepper. Serve at room temperature.

Makes about 1¾ cups

Each ¼ cup serving provides:

168	Calories	2 g	Carbohydrate
8 g	Protein	130 mg	Sodium
15 g	Fat	4 mg	Cholesterol

23

Creoja Sauce

Preparation time: 10 minutes (plus time to chill)

A spicy salsa from Brazil that goes especially well with barbecue. Good on fish and chicken.

3 tablespoons olive oil
4 tablespoons tomato sauce
1 tablespoon lemon juice
2 tablespoons red onion, finely chopped
2 tablespoons red bell pepper, finely chopped
2 tablespoons hot pepper, finely chopped (optional)
1 tablespoon fresh chives, chopped
1 tablespoon fresh cilantro, chopped
$^1/_8$ teaspoon pepper

Stir all ingredients together in a bowl. Chill thoroughly.

Makes about $^1/_2$ cup

Each 2 tablespoon serving provides:			
98	Calories	2 g	Carbohydrate
0 g	Protein	96 mg	Sodium
10 g	Fat	0 mg	Cholesterol

24

Spicy Pasta Sauce

Preparation time: 40 minutes

This different and spicy sauce is a great way to jazz up lasagna. You can also pour it over spaghetti or serve alongside sautéed vegetables.

¹/₄ cup olive oil
3 cloves garlic, minced
¹/₈ teaspoon cayenne
¹/₈ teaspoon crushed red pepper
¹/₂ teaspoon fresh oregano or ¹/₄ teaspoon dried
1 28-ounce can plum tomatoes, drained and chopped
1 tablespoon fresh parsley, minced

Over medium-high heat, bring everything except the parsley to a boil. Reduce heat and simmer 20 minutes, stirring occasionally. Stir in the parsley and simmer 5 minutes more.

Makes about 2 cups

Each ¹/₂ cup serving provides:

146	Calories	6 g	Carbohydrate
1 g	Protein	196 mg	Sodium
14 g	Fat	0 mg	Cholesterol

25

Carol's Meatless Bolognese

Preparation time: 1 1/2 hours

This sauce is an Italian original, by way of my friend Carol Bartley. Cook slowly, with plenty of stirring to prevent sticking, and you will be rewarded with a rich red sauce.

1/3 cup olive oil
6 cloves garlic, minced
1 small onion, minced
1 carrot, minced
1 stalk celery, minced
1 cup fresh parsley, chopped
1/4 cup water
1 large potato, grated
6 or 7 fresh Roma tomatoes or 1 28-ounce can, drained
1/8 teaspoon salt

Slowly sauté the garlic, onion, and carrot in olive oil until soft, stirring frequently. Add celery and parsley and continue to cook 5 minutes more. Add water and potato, stir to keep from sticking, then add tomatoes and salt to taste. Cook slowly, stirring often, covering occasionally, for about an hour. Add a little more water if the sauce cooks down.

Makes about 3 cups

Each 1/2 cup serving provides:

176	Calories	16 g	Carbohydrate
2 g	Protein	71 mg	Sodium
12 g	Fat	0 mg	Cholesterol

26

Herbed Tomato Sauce

Preparation time: 2 hours

Fresh oregano makes this pasta sauce best. Pour it over
your favorite noodles and Italian sausages.

1 28-ounce can tomatoes
5 cloves garlic, minced
1 small onion, minced
3 tablespoons fresh oregano or 3 teaspoons dried
1 teaspoon dried thyme
1 teaspoon dried marjoram
1 bay leaf
1 teaspoon pepper
1 cup dry red wine
1/2 cup fresh basil, torn or 1/4 cup dried
1/4 cup fresh parsley, chopped

Combine all ingredients except wine, basil, and parsley in
a large pot and bring to a boil. Reduce heat and simmer,
stirring occasionally, for 1 hour. Now add the wine, basil,
and parsley and cook 30 minutes longer.

Makes about 3 cups

Each 1/2 cup serving provides:

54	Calories	10 g	Carbohydrate
1 g	Protein	218 mg	Sodium
1 g	Fat	0 mg	Cholesterol

27

Cold Tomato-Basil Sauce

Preparation time: 15 minutes (plus time to chill)

This wonderful summer sauce is substantial enough to eat
alone as a cold soup. Or pour it over cooked and cooled
fresh vegetables, from cucumbers to carrots. Because of
the fresh nature of this recipe, you won't be as happy
with it if you resort to canned tomatoes. I also recom-
mend tearing fresh basil into small pieces rather than cut-
ting it since knives tend to turn basil black.

3 fresh tomatoes, peeled, seeded, and diced
1 tablespoon lemon juice
1 tablespoon dry red wine
1/8 cup extra-virgin olive oil
1/4 teaspoon fresh oregano, chopped
1/4 teaspoon salt
1/8 teaspoon pepper
Pinch of cayenne
3 tablespoons fresh basil, torn into small pieces

Puree tomatoes in a blender. Add lemon juice, wine, olive
oil, oregano, salt, pepper, and cayenne and pulse until
well-mixed. Remove to a bowl then stir in the basil. Serve
at room temperature or slightly chilled.

Makes about 1³/4 cups

Each 1/4 cup serving provides:

47	Calories	3 g	Carbohydrate
0 g	Protein	71 mg	Sodium
4 g	Fat	0 mg	Cholesterol

28

Italian Green Sauce

Preparation time: 10 minutes

This classic uncooked sauce is good with salads or fish.
Hard-boiled eggs have always been used as emulsifiers —
add at your option. If you want to turn it into a pasta
sauce, omit the egg and the vinegar, double the oil, and
puree until smooth.

²/₃ cup packed fresh basil leaves
¹/₃ cup packed fresh parsley
¹/₄ cup scallions, chopped
3 tablespoons fresh tarragon, chopped
1 large or 2 small cloves garlic, minced
1 tablespoon capers, drained
1 teaspoon salt
¹/₂ teaspoon pepper
1 hard-boiled egg, shelled and quartered (optional)
¹/₄ cup white wine vinegar
¹/₂ cup extra-virgin olive oil

Put all ingredients except oil and vinegar in a blender or
processor and chop or pulse to mix well, or puree but
leave some consistency. Remove to a bowl and whisk in
vinegar and then oil.

Makes about 2 cups

Each ¼ cup serving provides:			
137	Calories	2 g	Carbohydrate
1 g	Protein	300 mg	Sodium
14 g	Fat	27 mg	Cholesterol

29

Scallop Sauce

Preparation time: 10 minutes

My version of a common, quick, and delightful sauce available throughout Italy. Serve it over spaghettini or spaghetti.

1/2 cup extra-virgin olive oil
1 to 2 cloves garlic, minced
1 tablespoon parsley, chopped
Dash of cayenne
1/8 teaspoon salt
1 pound fresh scallops, cut into 1/4-inch pieces
1/4 cup plain bread crumbs, toasted

Sauté garlic in olive oil on low heat for 5 minutes. Add parsley, cayenne, and salt and stir, then add scallops. Turn heat to medium-high and cook for 1 minute, until scallops turn a flat white. Remove from heat and toss with pasta and bread crumbs.

Makes about 2 cups

Each 1/2 cup serving provides:

363	Calories	7 g	Carbohydrate
20 g	Protein	295 mg	Sodium
28 g	Fat	38 mg	Cholesterol

30

Salmoriglio Sauce

Preparation time: 10 minutes

This classic Sicilian sauce is a simple dressing for fish, especially halibut or swordfish.

1 teaspoon salt
2 tablespoons fresh lemon juice
1 teaspoon lemon zest
1 teaspoon fresh oregano or ½ teaspoon dried
⅓ cup olive oil
¼ teaspoon pepper

Dissolve salt in lemon juice then add lemon zest and oregano and stir. Slowly add oil, whisking it into lemon juice so that it blends in as you go. Add pepper, and pour sauce generously over cooked fish.

Makes about ½ cup

Each 2 tablespoon serving provides:

161	Calories	1 g	Carbohydrate
0 g	Protein	533 mg	Sodium
18 g	Fat	0 mg	Cholesterol

31

Piri-Piri Sauce

Preparation time: 45 minutes (plus 1 month storage time)

Piri-Piri is a very, very hot sauce, traditionally made in Portugal by scraping off part of a pepper and storing it in olive oil for 2 to 3 months. Piri-Piri, named after the Portuguese pepper (which actually is the malagueta, originally from Brazil), can be used in any way you might use Tabasco sauce. Carefully.

1 to 2 serrano or jalapeño peppers
1 cup warm water (to soak)
⅛ teaspoon salt
3 tablespoons wine vinegar
½ cup olive oil

Soak peppers in warm water for 30 minutes. Chop and seed, then season with salt. Put the peppers in an 8-ounce jar, add vinegar, then fill three-fourths of the way with oil. Store, sealed, for a month or more. Use with caution!

Makes ¾ cup

Each teaspoon serving provides:

26	Calories	0 g	Carbohydrate
0 g	Protein	0 mg	Sodium
3 g	Fat	0 mg	Cholesterol

32
Neapolitan Sauce

Preparation time: 40 minutes

This anchovy-tomato classic from Naples seems to be offered 100 ways by 100 cooks. Use on any pasta.

1/4 cup extra-virgin olive oil
3 cloves garlic, minced
1/2 cup Kalamata olives, pitted and halved
3 anchovy fillets, minced
1 tablespoon capers, drained
1 16-ounce can tomatoes or 1 pound fresh, peeled
    and seeded
1 tablespoon fresh oregano
1/4 cup tomato paste
1 tablespoon fresh basil, torn into small pieces
1/2 teaspoon pepper

Sauté garlic in olive oil on low heat 3 to 4 minutes. Add olives, anchovies, and capers and sauté on low-medium heat 6 to 7 minutes. Add remaining ingredients, except basil, and simmer 15 minutes. Add basil and simmer 5 minutes more.

Makes about 2 1/2 cups

Each 1/2 cup serving provides:

199	Calories	10 g	Carbohydrate
2 g	Protein	931 mg	Sodium
18 g	Fat	3 mg	Cholesterol

33

Lime, Basil, Chile Sauce

Preparation time: 10 minutes

This delightful sauce has a nice texture and aroma. Use it as a dip for uncooked vegetables such as broccoli, or spoon a little over ravioli.

³/₄ cup packed fresh basil leaves
2 tablespoons fresh lime juice
2 tablespoons mild chili pepper, minced
2 cloves garlic, minced
¹/₄ cup vegetable oil
Pinch of cayenne
¹/₄ teaspoon salt
¹/₄ teaspoon pepper

Blend all in blender or food processor until creamy.

Makes ³/₄ cup

	Each 2 tablespoon serving provides:		
84	Calories	1 g	Carbohydrate
0 g	Protein	78 mg	Sodium
9 g	Fat	0 mg	Cholesterol

34

Mexican Green Sauce

Preparation time: 30 minutes

Mexican food is my son Andrew's favorite, and it is for
him that I enjoy developing sauces for those foods. This
one is a pretty typical and versatile style of green sauce.
Pour it over burritos or, better yet, make a Mexican red
sauce and pour red on one end and green on the other. It
can be used in many Mexican dishes, including enchiladas and tacos.

1 pound fresh tomatillos (about 11), husked and
      washed
2 to 3 fresh green chiles—2 serranos and 1 jalapeño
      or for a very mild sauce 2 Anaheim peppers
5 sprigs fresh cilantro, coarsely chopped
5 fresh basil leaves, coarsely chopped (optional)
6 to 7 fresh mint leaves, coarsely chopped (optional)
1 small onion, chopped
1 clove garlic, chopped or minced
1 tablespoon vegetable oil
2 cups low-salt chicken broth
1/4 teaspoon salt

Boil tomatillos and chiles in salted water until just tender,
about 10 minutes, then drain. (If using canned tomatillos
or chiles simply drain.) Place in a blender or processor
with the cilantro, basil, mint, onion, and garlic and blend
until smooth. Heat oil in a skillet over medium-high heat.

continued next page

Pour all of the sauce in and stir for 5 minutes. Add broth, return to a boil, and reduce heat to medium. Simmer until thick, about 10 minutes.

Makes about 3 cups

Each ¹/₂ cup serving provides:

63	Calories	8 g	Carbohydrate
2 g	Protein	274 mg	Sodium
3 g	Fat	0 mg	Cholesterol

35

Quick, Mild Mexican Red Sauce

Preparation time: 10 minutes

Mexican Red takes only minutes to make. Put it in tacos,
on enchiladas, or pour over burritos. I like to grill chicken
strips on the barbecue, put them in a corn tortilla, add
fresh, cold cucumber slices, chopped onion, and a little
chopped cilantro, then pour on a little of this sauce.
Because dried herbs have different flavor than fresh, they
are preferred in this recipe.

1 28-ounce can tomatoes, drained well
2 mild canned green peppers, chopped
1 small onion, chopped
1 tablespoon dried oregano
1 tablespoon dried basil
1 tablespoon ground coriander
$^1/_2$ teaspoon crushed red pepper
$^1/_8$ teaspoon pepper
2 tablespoons vegetable oil
2 tablespoons fresh cilantro, chopped
$^1/_8$ teaspoon salt

Place the tomatoes, peppers, onion, oregano, basil,
coriander, red pepper, and pepper in a blender and puree.
Heat oil in a medium-high skillet. When hot, add puree

continued next page

to pan (it should be hot enough to sizzle) and stir, cooking for 4 to 5 minutes. Remove from heat, then add cilantro and salt.

Makes about 2 cups

Each ¹/₂ cup serving provides:

116	Calories	12 g	Carbohydrate
2 g	Protein	799 mg	Sodium
8 g	Fat	0 mg	Cholesterol

36

Avocado-Tomatillo Sauce

Preparation time: 15 minutes

This is a nice blend of avocado sweetness, balanced by a touch of tomatillo tartness. It will complement any cheese dish very well, such as quesadillas or enchiladas. Or use it as a dip for fresh vegetables.

7 to 8 tomatillos, husked and washed
2 to 3 avocados, skinned, chopped, and pitted
1/4 cup olive oil
Juice from 1/2 lemon
1/8 teaspoon cumin
2 cloves garlic, minced
1/2 cup onion, chopped
1/2 cup cilantro, chopped

Cook tomatillos in boiling water until soft, 7 to 8 minutes. Place all ingredients in a food processor or blender and puree. Serve immediately or chilled.

Makes about 3 1/2 cups

Each 1/4 cup serving provides:

86	Calories	3 g	Carbohydrate
1 g	Protein	5 mg	Sodium
8 g	Fat	0 mg	Cholesterol

37

Mild Surprise Two-Chile Sauce

Preparation time: 10 minutes (plus 8 to 12 hours marinating time)

For those of us who can't take the heat, but still can't get out of the kitchen, here is a mild chile sauce that gives the spicy flavor of chiles without the heat. This miracle is achieved through vinegar, which after a few hours robs the chiles of their fire. Great on the side of almost any Mexican dish or with meats.

4 Anaheim or New Mexican peppers
4 hot chili peppers
½ to ¾ cup vinegar
1 clove garlic, minced
2 tablespoons vegetable oil

Seed the peppers and slice into 1-inch pieces. Marinate peppers in vinegar for 8 to 12 hours, turning occasionally. Drain, then place the peppers in a blender along with ½ cup of fresh vinegar and the minced garlic. Puree, adding more vinegar to taste. Remove from blender and stir in vegetable oil. For a spicier sauce, pour the vinegar from the marinade into the blender rather than fresh vinegar.

Makes about 1 cup

Each 2 tablespoon serving provides:

50	Calories	5 g	Carbohydrate
1 g	Protein	3 mg	Sodium
3 g	Fat	0 mg	Cholesterol

38

Black Bean Sauce

Preparation time: 15 minutes

Many Cuban chefs use black beans in their sauces, and this jazzed-up version works well on ribs, shrimp, and chicken.

2 tablespoons vegetable oil
1 onion, chopped
1/2 red bell pepper, seeded and chopped
3 cloves garlic, minced
1 teaspoon fresh ginger, grated
3/4 cup cooked black beans
1/2 cup chicken broth
1/2 cup white wine
1 teaspoon soy sauce
1 teaspoon honey

Heat oil over low-medium heat and sauté onion, bell pepper, and garlic for 5 to 6 minutes, but do not brown. Add ginger, sauté 2 to 3 minutes, then add remaining ingredients. Simmer 3 to 4 minutes.

Makes about 3 cups

Each 1/4 cup serving provides:

50	Calories	5 g	Carbohydrate
1 g	Protein	60 mg	Sodium
2 g	Fat	0 mg	Cholesterol

39

Brazilian Salsa

Preparation time: 10 minutes (plus 1 hour standing time)

This hot sauce is a staple on tables in Brazil. It goes well with grilled meats, and can accompany vegetables. Brazilians use a malagueta pepper which is almost impossible to find in the United States. So substitute jalapeño or other hot pepper, to taste.

1 tablespoon fresh cilantro, minced
Juice from 3 limes
2 teaspoons onion, minced
1 teaspoon jalapeño or other hot pepper, minced
1 teaspoon fresh parsley, minced
$^1/_8$ teaspoon salt
$^1/_8$ teaspoon pepper

Mix all of the ingredients in a bowl and let stand for 1 hour. Serve at room temperature.

Makes about $^1/_2$ cup

Each 2 tablespoon serving provides:

7	Calories	2 g	Carbohydrate
0 g	Protein	67 mg	Sodium
0 g	Fat	0 mg	Cholesterol

40

Tomatillo Sauce

Preparation time: 20 minutes

The tart taste of the tomatillos sharpens up any Mexican dish, or any American grilled poultry or fish.

2 teaspoons olive oil
2 cloves garlic, minced
³/₄ pound tomatillos, husked, washed, and quartered
4 tablespoons lemon juice
³/₄ cup yellow or red bell pepper, seeded and
    chopped fine
1 to 2 tablespoons jalapeño or other hot pepper,
    chopped
¹/₄ cup cilantro, chopped
¹/₄ cup onion, finely chopped
¹/₄ teaspoon salt
¹/₈ teaspoon pepper

Sauté garlic in oil for 3 to 5 minutes. Add tomatillos to the pan with the lemon juice, bell pepper, and hot pepper. Cook over medium-high heat, stirring frequently, until tomatillos are bright green. Add remaining ingredients. Cool to room temperature before serving.

Makes about 3 cups

Each ¹/₄ cup serving provides:			
22	Calories	3 g	Carbohydrate
0 g	Protein	41 mg	Sodium
1 g	Fat	0 mg	Cholesterol

41

Sage-Chile Sauce

Preparation time: 40 minutes

A good shrimp sauce or spoon it over meat ravioli. This sauce's easygoing flavor arrives early but leaves with a great spicy aftertaste.

2 tablespoons vegetable oil
1 small onion, chopped
2 cloves garlic, minced
1 stalk celery, chopped
1/2 pound whole tomatillos, husked and washed
1 cup mild green chiles, chopped
1/8 cup serrano or other hot pepper, minced
3/4 cup low-salt chicken broth
3/4 cup water
2 teaspoons fresh sage or 1 teaspoon dried, crumbled
1/8 teaspoon cayenne

Heat oil and sauté onion, garlic, and celery until soft, about 5 minutes. Add remaining ingredients and bring to a boil. Simmer about 30 minutes, stirring frequently, removing the tomatillos as they soften. Place sauce in a blender and blend until smooth.

Makes about 2 cups

Each 1/4 cup serving provides:

54	Calories	5 g	Carbohydrate
1 g	Protein	297 mg	Sodium
4 g	Fat	0 mg	Cholesterol

42

Avocado Salsa

Preparation time: 15 minutes

For the avocado lover who doesn't want another guacamole, try this avocado salsa. Use it in any way you might use guacamole.

2 avocados, diced
2 tomatoes, diced
1 serrano chile, finely chopped
3 tablespoons lime juice
Zest of ½ lime
½ cup extra-virgin olive oil
1 tablespoon fresh cilantro, chopped
⅛ teaspoon salt
⅛ teaspoon pepper

Combine all ingredients in a bowl and mix well.

Makes about 3 cups

Each ¼ cup serving provides:

138	Calories	4 g	Carbohydrate
1 g	Protein	19 mg	Sodium
14 g	Fat	0 mg	Cholesterol

43

Tomatillo Mole

Preparation time: 20 minutes

This quick, mild salsa is good to cook fish or poultry in, to put into soups, or with enchilada or taco dishes.

1 pound fresh tomatillos, husked and washed
2 tablespoons canned green chiles, chopped
1 small onion, chopped
2 cloves garlic, minced
1/8 teaspoon cayenne
2 tablespoons cilantro, chopped
1/4 teaspoon salt

Boil tomatillos until just soft. Drain and place in a blender along with all other ingredients and blend until smooth. (If using to cook fish or poultry, thin with a little water or broth.)

Makes about 3 cups

Each 1/2 cup serving provides:

34	Calories	7 g	Carbohydrate
1 g	Protein	120 mg	Sodium
1 g	Fat	0 mg	Cholesterol

44

Avocado-Egg Sauce

Preparation time: 20 minutes

This spicy recipe is a Columbian staple, where it is served with steak or other beef and chicken dishes.

1 large avocado, pitted and mashed
1 hard-boiled egg yolk, mashed
1 hard-boiled egg white, finely chopped
1 small serrano or jalapeño pepper, seeded and finely chopped
1 tablespoon fresh cilantro, chopped
1 scallion, finely chopped
1 tablespoon lemon juice
1 teaspoon ground coriander
1/4 teaspoon salt
1/4 teaspoon pepper

Stir egg yolk and avocado together until well-mixed. Stir in and blend remaining ingredients.

Makes about 2 1/2 cups

	Each 1/4 cup serving provides:		
70	Calories	3 g	Carbohydrate
2 g	Protein	95 mg	Sodium
6 g	Fat	36 mg	Cholesterol

45

Lime Hot Sauce

Preparation time: 15 minutes

This Brazilian sauce is good with meat, poultry, or fish. Brazilians use malagueta peppers which are very hot. Substitute to your taste.

1 clove garlic, chopped
1/2 onion, finely chopped
3 serrano or jalapeño peppers, seeded and finely
    chopped
1/4 teaspoon salt
1/2 cup fresh lime juice
1 teaspoon lemon zest
1 tablespoon fresh cilantro, chopped

Puree garlic, onion, and peppers in a food processor. Add salt, lime juice, and zest and blend. Sprinkle with cilantro. This can be prepared in a mortar by crushing the first four ingredients then slowly adding the lemon juice and zest.

Makes about 3/4 cup

Each tablespoon serving provides:

10	Calories	3 g	Carbohydrate
0 g	Protein	41 mg	Sodium
0 g	Fat	0 mg	Cholesterol

46

Guacamole Salsa

Preparation time: 15 minutes

Use this with Mexican foods, especially quesadillas.

4 fresh tomatillos, husked and rinsed
1 clove garlic, chopped
1/3 cup cilantro, chopped
1 serrano pepper, chopped
1 1/2 avocados
1 teaspoon Mexican oregano
3 tablespoons white or red onion, minced
2 tablespoons lemon juice
1/4 cup olive oil
1/4 teaspoon salt

Just soften the tomatillos in boiling water, about 4 to 5 minutes, then remove to a bowl and quarter. Mix with garlic and cilantro, then add pepper, avocado, and oregano. Stir in onion, lemon juice, olive oil, and salt.

Makes about 3 cups

Each 1/4 cup serving provides:

86	Calories	3 g	Carbohydrate
1 g	Protein	44 mg	Sodium
8 g	Fat	0 mg	Cholesterol

47

Gazpacho Sauce

Preparation time: 20 minutes (plus 1 hour to chill)

My mother makes great gazpacho. It must be the southern Irish in her. I use a hand chopper rather than a blender or processor for this, since you don't want it pureed, just finely chopped. Try this with fish or grilled chicken, or add to Mexican dishes.

½ cucumber, peeled, seeded and minced
½ green bell pepper, seeded and minced
½ red bell pepper, seeded and minced
1 cup tomatoes, skinned, seeded, and cubed
2 stalks celery, minced
1 scallion, finely chopped
2 cloves garlic, minced
2 tablespoons parsley, finely chopped
1 tablespoon basil, torn into small pieces
Juice from 1 lemon
2 tablespoons extra-virgin olive oil
¼ teaspoon salt
¼ teaspoon pepper

Drain the vegetables that need it, then toss all ingredients together in a bowl and chill for 1 hour.

Makes about 3 cups

Each ¼ cup serving provides:

30	Calories	2 g	Carbohydrate
0 g	Protein	48 mg	Sodium
2 g	Fat	0 mg	Cholesterol

48

Salsa Ranchera

Preparation time: 15 minutes (plus 1 hour standing time)

This tomato salsa is the most popular of fresh Mexican salsas, accompanying everything from eggs to enchiladas. My version is especially mild — toss in a chopped jalapeño if you like it hot.

1 pablano chile, finely chopped
2 tomatoes, roasted and peeled
1 red onion, finely chopped
1 clove garlic, minced
1/4 teaspoon oregano (Mexican recommended)
1/4 teaspoon marjoram, chopped
1/8 teaspoon ground cumin
1/4 teaspoon salt
1 tablespoon extra-virgin olive oil
1 teaspoon lemon juice

Toss all ingredients together. You may want to let it stand for an hour to blend the flavors.

Makes about 2 cups

Each 1/4 cup serving provides:

33	Calories	4 g	Carbohydrate
1 g	Protein	70 mg	Sodium
2 g	Fat	0 mg	Cholesterol

49

Black Bean Salsa

Preparation time: 10 minutes (plus 30 minutes standing time)

Here's a simple, quick, and mild salsa with a good blend of flavors to use with chips, or with grilled meats, or Mexican foods.

2 cups black beans, cooked and drained
¹/₄ to ¹/₂ jalapeño chile, roasted, peeled, seeded, and
    chopped
Juice from 1 lime
¹/₂ cup jicama, chopped
1¹/₂ tablespoons cilantro, chopped
¹/₂ red or white onion, finely chopped
¹/₈ teaspoon cumin
¹/₈ teaspoon salt
¹/₄ teaspoon pepper

Mix all ingredients in a bowl and let sit for 30 minutes.

Makes about 2³/₄ cups

Each ¹/₄ cup serving provides:

46	Calories	9 g	Carbohydrate
3 g	Protein	14 mg	Sodium
0 g	Fat	0 mg	Cholesterol

50

Parsley-Tarragon Sauce

Preparation time: 10 minutes

The parsley and tarragon flavors go well with vegetables, especially cooked carrots. It can double as a dressing over greens. Use sparingly to enhance, not overwhelm, the food.

1 tablespoon Dijon mustard
1 teaspoon tarragon vinegar
3 tablespoons fresh parsley, finely chopped
1 teaspoon fresh tarragon or ¹/₂ teaspoon dried
3 tablespoons extra-virgin olive oil
¹/₂ teaspoon lemon juice

Mix mustard, vinegar, parsley, and tarragon in a bowl. Slowly add the olive oil, whisking it in to mix. Add lemon juice, whisk thoroughly.

Makes about ¹/₂ cup

Each tablespoon serving provides:

49	Calories	0 g	Carbohydrate
0 g	Protein	51 mg	Sodium
5 g	Fat	0 mg	Cholesterol

51

Herbed Aioli

Preparation time: 10 minutes

Aioli, a sort of French mayonnaise, is a staple in
Provence. It's delicious but can be a little too vigorous for
American tastes. Herbed aioli is a nice way to bring out
the flavors of tarragon, rosemary, or basil. Put a dollop of
any flavor aioli on steamed vegetables. Rosemary aioli is
especially good on lamb; tarragon or basil aioli goes well
with most fish.

3 cloves garlic, minced
2 egg yolks
3 tablespoons lemon juice
1¼ to 1½ cups extra-virgin olive oil
¼ teaspoon salt
1 tablespoon tarragon, rosemary, or basil, finely chopped

Combine garlic, egg yolks, and lemon juice in a blender or
processor and process until smooth. Slowly pour in a
stream of olive oil to desired consistency. Whisk in salt
and your chosen herb.

Makes about 2 cups

Each tablespoon serving provides:			
79	Calories	0 g	Carbohydrate
0 g	Protein	14 mg	Sodium
9 g	Fat	13 mg	Cholesterol

52

Tapenade

Preparation time: 15 minutes

Provençal pungent, this French staple is good on bread, in omelets, with tomatoes, or with meats—it will enliven any bland foods. You can use Italian or Greek olives in place of Niçoise, but rinse off the salt first if you do.

1 cup Niçoise olives, pitted
2 tablespoons capers, drained
6 to 7 fresh basil leaves
1 clove garlic, minced
1/2 teaspoon fresh thyme or 1/4 teaspoon dried
1 tablespoon lemon juice
1/2 teaspoon freshly ground pepper
3 tablespoons olive oil

Put everything except the olive oil in food processor and just chop. Add olive oil in a stream with the machine running.

Makes about 1/4 cup

Each 2 tablespoon serving provides:

85	Calories	2 g	Carbohydrate
0 g	Protein	465 mg	Sodium
9 g	Fat	0 mg	Cholesterol

53

Peanut or Cashew Sauce

Preparation time: 5 minutes

This sauce is for Oriental, including Thai, dishes. Try it over eggplant as well.

½ cup peanut or cashew butter
1 clove garlic, minced
¼ cup honey
2 tablespoons lemon juice
Pinch of cinnamon
¼ cup soy sauce
1 teaspoon rice vinegar
1 teaspoon fresh ginger, grated
Pinch of crushed red pepper
¼ cup water if needed

Blend all ingredients in a blender. Add water if needed.

Makes about 1 cup

Each 2 tablespoon serving provides:

133	Calories	13 g	Carbohydrate
4 g	Protein	592 mg	Sodium
8 g	Fat	0 mg	Cholesterol

54

Cucumber Raita

Preparation time: 10 minutes (plus time to chill)

This traditional Indian sauce or condiment is usually served with curried foods. Use for cooling off spicy foods.

$1/2$ teaspoon whole cumin seeds
1 cucumber, peeled, seeded, and coarsely grated
3 cups nonfat or lowfat yogurt
1 teaspoon salt
$1/4$ teaspoon fresh ginger, grated
Dash of cayenne
Mint leaves for garnish

Roast whole cumin seeds in a pan in a hot oven 4 to 5 minutes, stirring frequently. Cool, then grind them—a coffee grinder will usually work or use a mortar and pestle. Combine all ingredients and chill. Garnish with mint leaves.

Makes about 4 cups

Each $1/2$ cup serving provides:

52	Calories	7 g	Carbohydrate
5 g	Protein	333 mg	Sodium
0 g	Fat	2 mg	Cholesterol

55

Yogurt-Orange Sauce

Preparation time: 10 minutes

This is especially good over fruit, with curried dishes (use instead of a raita), or with cold cucumbers.

1/4 cup fresh orange juice
1/2 teaspoon orange zest
1/4 cup canola oil
1/2 cup nonfat or lowfat yogurt
2 teaspoons fresh dill, chopped
2 teaspoons fresh cilantro, chopped
1/2 teaspoon fresh parsley, chopped

Combine juice, zest, and oil until well-blended. Stir in yogurt. Add herbs just before serving.

Makes about 1 cup

Each 1/4 cup serving provides:

148	Calories	4 g	Carbohydrate
2 g	Protein	23 mg	Sodium
14 g	Fat	1 mg	Cholesterol

56

Yogurt-Curry Sauce

Preparation time: 15 minutes

This curry is mild enough for children to enjoy since there is just a touch of a bite from the cayenne, yet its spiciness is complex enough for adults. You can substitute 3 1/2 teaspoons of curry powder for the cayenne, cumin, cardamom, coriander, turmeric, paprika, and cinnamon, with varying results, depending on the blend of curry powder used.

Cook a skinless breast of chicken with cashews in the same pan you used for the sauce for a quick, delicious entree, or stir a little of this sauce into rice with warmed raisins. It will keep in the refrigerator for a few days, but it is at its best fresh from the stove.

2 tablespoons vegetable oil
1 red (or yellow) onion, finely chopped
1 1/2 tablespoons fresh ginger, finely chopped
1/8 teaspoon cayenne
1/4 teaspoon cumin
1 teaspoon ground cardamom
1 teaspoon ground coriander
1/2 teaspoon turmeric
1 teaspoon paprika
1/4 teaspoon cinnamon
1/8 teaspoon salt
1/2 cup yogurt

continued next page

Place onion and ginger in vegetable oil over medium heat. Add spices and stir frequently for 5 minutes. Move the onion mixture into a blender, add yogurt, and mix well.

Makes about 1¹/₂ cups

Each ¹/₄ cup serving provides:

66	Calories	5 g	Carbohydrate
2 g	Protein	55 mg	Sodium
5 g	Fat	0 mg	Cholesterol

57

Pineapple-Curry Sauce

Preparation time: 10 minutes

This has sweet and tangy flavors that go well with ham or chicken, or over rice. If it is too sweet for your taste, add a dash of cayenne.

1/4 teaspoon each cardamom, turmeric, ground
    coriander, cumin
1/8 teaspoon each ground cloves, nutmeg
1/2 teaspoon paprika
2 cloves garlic, minced
1 1/2 teaspoons fresh ginger, grated
1 tablespoon brown sugar
1/4 cup pineapple juice
1/2 cup pineapple, finely diced

Stir spices together in a small skillet on low heat for a minute or two. Add garlic, ginger, sugar, and pineapple juice and cook on medium heat, stirring frequently, for 5 to 7 minutes. Remove from heat and add diced pineapple.

Makes about 1 cup

Each 2 tablespoon serving provides:

27	Calories	7 g	Carbohydrate
0 g	Protein	1 mg	Sodium
0 g	Fat	0 mg	Cholesterol

58

Soy-Ginger Sauce

Preparation time: 5 minutes (plus 30 minutes standing time)

This makes a nice sauce for vegetables, especially those accompanying Asian dishes, or use it on a tuna steak. Tamari is recommended over soy sauce because of its more balanced flavor.

¼ cup tamari or soy sauce
¼ cup water
1 teaspoon sherry
1 tablespoon fresh ginger, grated
1 teaspoon vegetable oil
½ teaspoon sugar

Whisk all ingredients together, then let stand for 30 minutes. Before serving, strain to remove ginger strings.

Makes about ³/₄ cup

Each 2 tablespoon serving provides:

18	Calories	1 g	Carbohydrate
1 g	Protein	671 mg	Sodium
1 g	Fat	0 mg	Cholesterol

59

Japanese Yellow Sauce

Preparation time: 15 minutes (plus time to chill)

This Japanese sauce works well as a dipping sauce for
fish and vegetables.

1/4 cup rice vinegar
1/8 cup sugar
1/8 teaspoon salt
3 egg yolks

Gently heat the first three ingredients in a saucepan until
the sugar and salt melt. Cool to room temperature, then
remove 1 tablespoon of the mixture and set aside. Stir egg
yolks into the pan and place over high heat for very short
intervals, stirring constantly. The trick is to bring out the
sauce's bright color without scorching or curdling the
ingredients. This should take about 90 seconds — heating
the sauce for 5 to 10 seconds at a time then cooling the pan
on a damp towel for an equal amount of time. Don't worry
about lumps. Transfer the cooked sauce to a napkin or
linen towel. Gather up the ends and twist, forcing the sauce
through the towel into a bowl. Add the tablespoon you set
aside to achieve desired consistency. Chill before serving.

Makes about 1/2 cup

Each 2 tablespoon serving provides:			
67	Calories	6 g	Carbohydrate
2 g	Protein	73 mg	Sodium
4 g	Fat	159 mg	Cholesterol

60

Baba Ghannouj

Preparation time: 55 minutes

The key to creating this Lebanese appetizer is making
sure the eggplant has been cooked completely. Scoop it
into pita bread, serve it with vegetables, or use as a dipping sauce for crudités. Tahini is a sesame seed paste
available in most markets.

1½ pounds eggplant
⅓ cup lemon juice
⅓ cup tahini
2 cloves garlic, minced
2 teaspoons extra-virgin olive oil
½ teaspoon paprika

Pierce eggplant with a fork, place on foil in a 400° oven for
40 to 45 minutes, or until very soft. Cool, then peel and
remove seeds. Put the eggplant in a food processor and
sprinkle with lemon juice. Add tahini and garlic and process
until smooth. Spread onto a serving plate and pour a little
olive oil over it, then give it a light dusting of paprika.

Makes 3 cups

Each ¼ cup serving provides:

64	Calories	6 g	Carbohydrate
2 g	Protein	9 mg	Sodium
4 g	Fat	0 mg	Cholesterol

61

Harissa

Preparation time: 10 minutes

There are as many recipes for harissa as there are cooks in Morroco I suppose, where this fiery sauce originated. My version has a little less fire than others, but it is still hot. In the Middle East harissa is often served with cous-cous and other bland foods. But you can try it with bar-becued chicken or any dish where you might enjoy a very hot sauce.

8 hot peppers (¹/₃ to ¹/₂ cup), stemmed, seeded, and
    chopped
1 teaspoon caraway seeds
4 cloves garlic, peeled
¹/₃ cup olive oil
¹/₄ teaspoon salt

Put all ingredients in a blender and puree.

Makes about ³/₄ cup

Each tablespoon serving provides:

65	Calories	3 g	Carbohydrate
1 g	Protein	42 mg	Sodium
6 g	Fat	0 mg	Cholesterol

62

Ravigote

Preparation time: 5 minutes

This Mediterranean classic has many different versions
and all are served with cold meats, poultry, or fish. Try it
as a dip with meats or vegetables.

$^1/_2$ cup olive oil
$^1/_8$ cup wine vinegar
1 teaspoon lemon juice
$^1/_2$ teaspoon Dijon mustard
$^1/_2$ teaspoon each parsley, scallion, and tarragon,
    minced
$^1/_2$ small white onion, finely diced
1 teaspoon capers, drained

Blend all in a bowl.

Makes $^3/_4$ cup

Each 2 tablespoon serving provides:

165	Calories	1 g	Carbohydrate
0 g	Protein	20 mg	Sodium
18 g	Fat	0 mg	Cholesterol

63

Charmoula

Preparation time: 10 minutes (plus ¹/₂ hour marinating time)

This is a traditional fish marinade from North Africa. I find it a piquant sauce as well, for fish, vegetables, and even potatoes. If using as a marinade you might want to add ¹/₂ cup of fresh cilantro. Let it rest ¹/₂ hour if using as a dip or sauce.

5 cloves garlic, minced
¹/₄ cup lemon juice
1 tablespoon tomato paste
¹/₂ teaspoon salt
1 tablespoon paprika
1 teaspoon cumin
Pinch of cayenne
¹/₄ teaspoon pepper

Place all ingredients in a blender or processor until finely chopped. Brush sparingly on fish and marinate for ¹/₂ hour.

Makes about ³/₄ cup

Each 2 tablespoon serving provides:

12	Calories	3 g	Carbohydrate
1 g	Protein	185 mg	Sodium
0 g	Fat	0 mg	Cholesterol

64

Tzatziki Sauce

Preparation time: 10 minutes (plus time to chill)

Tzatziki, the well-known Greek dipping sauce with the
cool flavors, is great with cold vegetables. Mint is more
traditional for the dish, but I prefer cilantro. This version
is also great on sandwiches and cools spicy dishes.

1 cucumber, peeled, seeded, and minced
2 cups nonfat or lowfat yogurt
1 small clove garlic, minced
1½ tablespoons red wine vinegar
¼ teaspoon fresh cilantro (or mint), finely chopped
¼ teaspoon salt
¼ teaspoon white pepper

Finely chop or mince the cucumber. Combine all ingredients in a bowl and chill.

Makes about 3 cups

Each ¼ cup serving provides:

26	Calories	4 g	Carbohydrate
2 g	Protein	70 mg	Sodium
0 g	Fat	1 mg	Cholesterol

65

Skordalia

Preparation time: 40 to 60 minutes

This has been a Mediterranean favorite since the days of
ancient Greece. It is robust, thus a good match for the
strong flavors of the region, and goes especially well with
fish and vegetable dishes.

1 pound potatoes (about 3 medium Russets)
1 egg yolk
6 cloves garlic, minced
$^1/_2$ cup olive oil
Juice from 2 lemons
$^1/_2$ teaspoon salt
$^1/_4$ teaspoon pepper

Boil potatoes, with skins, for about 20 minutes or bake 45
minutes in a 350° oven, until soft. Cool, then peel and
mash with a fork. Place potatoes in a mortar or bowl, add
egg yolk and garlic, and pound to smooth. Add oil a little
at a time, blending and pounding. Stir in lemon juice and
seasonings. Serve within 3 hours.

Makes about 4 cups

Each $^1/_4$ cup serving provides:

91	Calories	7 g	Carbohydrate
1 g	Protein	69 mg	Sodium
7 g	Fat	13 mg	Cholesterol

66

Cucumber Sauce

Preparation time: 5 minutes (plus time to chill)

I use cucumber as a refresher to otherwise hot dishes. I toss cukes into tacos, or serve on the side bathed in vinegar and dill. This cold cucumber sauce nicely offsets Mediterranean dishes, and goes well with lamb or eggplant.

1 cucumber, peeled, seeded, and finely chopped
1 cup nonfat or lowfat yogurt
Juice from ½ lemon
1 tablespoon parsley, chopped
1 tablespoon fresh dill, chopped
Scant ⅛ teaspoon salt

Combine all ingredients, and chill.

Makes about 2 cups

Each ¼ cup serving provides:

23	Calories	4 g	Carbohydrate
2 g	Protein	50 mg	Sodium
0 g	Fat	1 mg	Cholesterol

67

Almond-Coriander Sauce

Preparation time: 10 minutes

This sauce is delicious with meats, fish, or vegetables, especially with Greek dishes, such as souvlaki.

¹/₄ cup ground almonds
¹/₄ teaspoon ground coriander
1 teaspoon sugar
1 clove garlic, minced
Juice from 1 lemon
³/₄ cup nonfat or lowfat yogurt
¹/₈ teaspoon salt
¹/₈ teaspoon pepper
¹/₈ cup Italian parsley, chopped
¹/₄ cup cilantro, chopped

Put all ingredients except cilantro and parsley in a blender. Remove to bowl and stir them in.

Makes about 1³/₄ cups

Each ¹/₄ cup serving provides:

56	Calories	5 g	Carbohydrate
3 g	Protein	48 mg	Sodium
3 g	Fat	0 mg	Cholesterol

68

Tarator

Preparation time: 5 minutes

This Mediterranean classic is often called pine nut sauce, especially in Greece. However, the Turks like to make it with walnuts and Syrians prefer almonds, while hazelnuts and even pistachios are used in other recipes from the region. Enjoy it with poached or baked fish (you can put it on before cooking if you wish) or with vegetables.

1 cup pine or other nut, shelled
2 cloves garlic, minced
4 tablespoons tahini
3 tablespoons red wine vinegar
Pinch of cayenne
2 tablespoons olive oil, fish stock, clam juice, or
      broth from the dish to be sauced

Place all ingredients except oil in a blender and process until smooth. Use enough oil or other liquid to thin to consistency of yogurt.

Makes about 1³/₄ cups

Each 2 tablespoon serving provides:

100	Calories	3 g	Carbohydrate
3 g	Protein	5 mg	Sodium
10 g	Fat	0 mg	Cholesterol

69

Mint Pesto

Preparation time: 7 minutes

When I was growing up my mother frequently fixed leg of lamb for Sunday dinner, which she served along with mint jelly. Mint is wonderful with lamb, and this pesto is perfect. Just don't expect to be able to go back to mint jelly ever again.

1 cup packed fresh mint leaves
$1/2$ cup fresh Italian parsley
1 large clove garlic, minced
$1/2$ cup walnuts or pine nuts, chopped
$1/2$ cup extra-virgin olive oil
$1/8$ teaspoon salt
$1/8$ teaspoon pepper

Blend all ingredients in a food processor or blender until almost smooth, keeping a little bit of texture.

Makes 1$1/2$ to 2 cups

Each 2 tablespoon serving provides:

85	Calories	1 g	Carbohydrate
1 g	Protein	16 mg	Sodium
9 g	Fat	0 mg	Cholesterol

70

Cajun in a Hurry

Preparation time: 25 minutes

This quick Creole sauce is nicely tangy on poultry, omelets, fish, or fresh vegetables.

$^1/_8$ cup olive oil
$^1/_2$ onion, finely chopped
$^1/_2$ green or red bell pepper, finely chopped
1 stalk celery, finely chopped
2 cloves garlic, minced
$^1/_4$ teaspoon paprika
$^1/_2$ teaspoon ground coriander
$^1/_8$ teaspoon cayenne
$^1/_8$ teaspoon chili powder
$^1/_2$ teaspoon dried basil
1 teaspoon fresh thyme or $^1/_2$ teaspoon dried
$^1/_8$ teaspoon pepper
$^1/_2$ cup chicken broth
$^1/_2$ cup tomato sauce
$^1/_8$ teaspoon Tabasco sauce

Heat oil in a large skillet, then add onion, peppers, celery, and garlic. Add seasonings and mix well. Sauté over low heat, stirring occasionally, until onion and peppers are soft, about 5 minutes. Add remaining ingredients, increase heat to boil, then simmer uncovered until sauce thickens, about 15 minutes.

Makes about 1$^3/_4$ cups

Each ¼ cup serving provides:

50	Calories	3 g	Carbohydrate
1 g	Protein	162 mg	Sodium
4 g	Fat	0 mg	Cholesterol

71

Orange Sauce

Preparation time: 10 minutes

I grew up in southern California where our backyard featured both an orange tree and an avocado tree. We could sell the avocados for a nickel, but not the oranges. Perhaps everyone else had a yard full of them too. This sauce has a wonderfully rich flavor that goes very well with meats, especially ham and pork.

1 teaspoon brown sugar
1 teaspoon cornstarch
1 tablespoon lemon juice
1 cup fresh orange juice
$^{1}/_{4}$ teaspoon allspice
$^{1}/_{8}$ teaspoon nutmeg

Dissolve brown sugar and cornstarch in lemon juice, then place in a saucepan with the orange juice. Bring to a boil and simmer until thickened, about 2 minutes, stirring frequently. Add spices and stir on medium heat for a minute more.

Makes about 1¹/₂ cups

Each ¹/₄ cup serving provides:

24	Calories	6 g	Carbohydrate
0 g	Protein	1 mg	Sodium
0 g	Fat	0 mg	Cholesterol

72

Mushroom Sauce

Preparation time: 30 minutes

The Northwest is mushroom country, and this versatile sauce is wonderful on meats or vegetables. Use fresh crimini or button mushrooms.

1 onion, minced
1 tablespoon sesame or walnut oil
1 tablespoon olive oil
Scant $1/4$ cup pastry flour
$3/4$ cup heated vegetable or chicken broth or water
$1/4$ pound fresh mushrooms, sliced
$1/8$ teaspoon dried tarragon
$1/4$ teaspoon fresh parsley, chopped
$1/8$ teaspoon salt
$1/8$ teaspoon pepper

Sauté onions in the oils over medium heat until soft, about 5 minutes. Add flour and stir for 6 to 7 minutes. Remove from heat and whisk in the stock or water, whisking until the sauce thickens. Return to heat, add mushrooms, herbs, salt, and pepper and cook over low heat, stirring occasionally, for 10 to 15 minutes.

Makes about 2 cups

Each $1/4$ cup serving provides:

61	Calories	6 g	Carbohydrate
2 g	Protein	101 mg	Sodium
4 g	Fat	0 mg	Cholesterol

73

Creamy Almond Sauce

Preparation time: 10 minutes

This mild sauce is good on chicken and over rice. Dried ginger has a different taste than fresh ginger, and dried is recommended for this sauce.

$1/3$ cup almonds, toasted
$1/2$ cup apple juice
1 teaspoon lemon juice
$1/4$ teaspoon lemon zest
$1/8$ teaspoon dried ginger
$3/4$ cup vegetable or chicken broth

Combine everything except the broth in a blender and don't overprocess. In a skillet, boil the broth then stir in the almond mixture and simmer 3 to 4 minutes.

Makes about $1^3/4$ cups

Each $1/4$ cup serving provides:			
51	Calories	4 g	Carbohydrate
1 g	Protein	108 mg	Sodium
3 g	Fat	0 mg	Cholesterol

74

Walnut-Dill Sauce

Preparation time: 5 minutes

Fresh dill goes well with fish sauces, and this one is especially good on salmon and tuna. You might also try it with chicken. Make it with fresh dill only.

3/4 cup yogurt
1/4 teaspoon salt
2 teaspoons fresh dill, chopped
1/4 teaspoon tarragon
1/2 teaspoon vinegar
1 teaspoon lemon juice
2 teaspoons walnut oil
1 teaspoon plus 1 tablespoon walnuts, chopped
    and toasted

Combine all ingredients except 1 tablespoon of chopped walnuts in a blender and blend until smooth. Top with chopped walnuts.

Makes about 1 cup

Each 1/4 cup serving provides:

61	Calories	4 g	Carbohydrate
3 g	Protein	167 mg	Sodium
4 g	Fat	1 mg	Cholesterol

75

Orange Salsa

Preparation time: 10 minutes

This recipe, passed along to me by Wendy Kruetner, is terrific with grilled chicken.

1/2 cup dry white wine
1 clove garlic, finely chopped
3 scallions, chopped
1/4 cup red pepper, chopped
1/4 cup green pepper, chopped
1 orange, peeled and chopped
1 tablespoon fresh cilantro, chopped

Cook garlic, scallions, and peppers in white wine until just soft, about 5 minutes over low heat. Add orange and cilantro until warm. Remove from heat and pour over chicken.

Makes about 1³/4 cups

Each 2 tablespoon serving provides:

11	Calories	2 g	Carbohydrate
0 g	Protein	1 mg	Sodium
0 g	Fat	0 mg	Cholesterol

76

Rosemary Sauce

Preparation time: 15 minutes

Try this on vegetables, such as broccoli or cauliflower, or serve it with fish.

1 cup flour
$\frac{1}{2}$ cup white wine vinegar
$1\frac{1}{4}$ cups hot water
2 cloves garlic, minced
3 tablespoons fresh rosemary, minced
$\frac{1}{8}$ teaspoon salt

Make a dry roux by placing flour in a skillet and cooking over low heat. Stir and scrape the flour until it is very light brown, about 5 to 7 minutes. Continue to stir and add remaining ingredients in the order given. Simmer, stirring occasionally, about 5 minutes until it thickens.

Makes about 2 cups

Each $\frac{1}{4}$ cup serving provides:

63	Calories	14 g	Carbohydrate
2 g	Protein	29 mg	Sodium
0 g	Fat	0 mg	Cholesterol

77

Ginger-Tomato Sauce

Preparation time: 25 minutes

The hint of ginger flavor nicely offsets the naturally tart taste of tomatoes. Serve with chicken or fish.

3 tablespoons extra-virgin olive oil
1 small onion, minced
1½ teaspoons ginger, freshly grated
1 14-ounce can tomatoes, minced, with juice
Scant ⅛ teaspoon salt

Cook onion in oil until softened, then add 1 teaspoon of the ginger. Cook for a minute or two over low heat, add the tomatoes, juice and salt, increase heat and simmer, stirring frequently, until thickened, about 15 minutes. About 5 minutes before finished, add the remaining ½ teaspoon of ginger.

Makes about 2 cups

Each ¼ cup serving provides:

62	Calories	4 g	Carbohydrate
0 g	Protein	113 mg	Sodium
5 g	Fat	0 mg	Cholesterol

78

Carrot-Cilantro Sauce

Preparation time: 15 minutes (plus time to chill)

This may seem like an unusual combination but carrots are really quite versatile in making sauces, and the cilantro complements the carrot flavor nicely. Try it with chicken or fish.

2 cups carrots, peeled and sliced
3 to 4 tablespoons water
1 teaspoon fresh lemon juice
³/₄ cup nonfat or lowfat yogurt
2 tablespoons fresh cilantro, minced
¹/₂ teaspoon honey
¹/₈ teaspoon salt

Boil carrots until very tender. Remove from heat and puree in blender or processor with water until smooth. Stir in remaining ingredients. Chill before serving.

Makes about 2¹/₂ cups

Each ¹/₄ cup serving provides:

26	Calories	5 g	Carbohydrate
1 g	Protein	48 mg	Sodium
0 g	Fat	0 mg	Cholesterol

79

Lemon-Dill Cream Sauce

Preparation time: 10 minutes

This refreshing lemony sauce is good on artichokes, zucchini, or as a dipping sauce for fish.

2 tablespoons lemon juice
2 tablespoons fresh dill, finely chopped
1/4 cup nonfat or lowfat yogurt
1 tablespoon honey
1/8 cup milk

Mix lemon juice and dill. In a separate bowl, mix the yogurt, honey, and milk. Stir the two together.

Makes about 3/4 cup

Each 2 tablespoon serving provides:

21	Calories	4 g	Carbohydrate
1 g	Protein	10 mg	Sodium
0 g	Fat	1 mg	Cholesterol

80

Creamy Mushroom Sauce

Preparation time: 45 minutes

Delicious with pasta or with poultry, what this sauce lacks in appearance (rather dull), it more than makes up for in taste. You may make it more attractive by topping with fresh sliced mushrooms and parsley.

1/4 cup onion, minced
1/4 cup carrot, minced
4 cloves garlic, minced
1/4 cup olive oil
1/4 teaspoon cardamom
1/4 teaspoon turmeric
1/4 teaspoon fresh ginger, grated
1/4 teaspoon ground coriander
Pinch of cayenne
Scant 1/8 teaspoon salt
3 cups low-salt chicken broth
1 cup dry white wine
3 cups mushrooms, chopped
2 tablespoons scallion, chopped
2 teaspoons white wine vinegar
Fresh sliced mushrooms and parsley for garnish

In half of the olive oil cook the onion, carrot, and 1 garlic clove over low heat until soft, about 5 minutes. Add seasonings, cook a minute or two longer, then add the broth and wine and bring to a boil. Reduce heat and simmer for 15 minutes.

continued next page

In another skillet, sauté mushrooms in the remaining oil for about 5 minutes. Add scallion and remaining garlic and sauté another 3 to 4 minutes. Add broth from the first pot and simmer until reduced by about one fourth. Transfer to a blender, add white wine vinegar, and puree. Garnish if you wish.

Makes 2 to 2¹/₂ cups

Each ¹/₂ cup serving provides:

134	Calories	5 g	Carbohydrate
2 g	Protein	401 mg	Sodium
12 g	Fat	0 mg	Cholesterol

81

Snappy Chicken Sauce

Preparation time: 30 minutes

This sauce works well poured over leftover chicken but is even better when skinless breasts are cooked right in the sauce. Add the breasts when the sauce is about 5 minutes from being done.

1 tablespoon olive oil
1 small onion, finely chopped
1 tomato, seeded and chopped
$\frac{1}{2}$ cup chicken broth
3 cloves garlic, minced
$\frac{1}{2}$ teaspoon dried thyme
$\frac{1}{2}$ teaspoon dried tarragon
2 teaspoons white wine vinegar
$\frac{1}{8}$ teaspoon pepper

Cook onion in oil until soft, about 5 minutes. Add remaining ingredients and simmer 10 to 15 minutes.

Makes about 1 cup

Each $\frac{1}{4}$ cup serving provides:

57	Calories	5 g	Carbohydrate
1 g	Protein	104 mg	Sodium
4 g	Fat	0 mg	Cholesterol

82

Almond Pesto

Preparation time: 15 minutes

Try this with fish, chicken, or vegetables. Make it just
before you use it, since it doesn't keep well, not even for
one day.

1/2 cup almonds, toasted and chopped
1 clove garlic, minced
1/4 cup olive oil
1 tablespoon white wine vinegar
Pinch of cayenne

Toast almonds in a 300° oven until the skins begin to
crack, about 10 minutes. Cool, then finely chop. Mix
together remaining ingredients, then add the almonds.

Makes about 3/4 cup

Each 2 tablespoon serving provides:

145	Calories	3 g	Carbohydrate
2 g	Protein	1 mg	Sodium
15 g	Fat	0 mg	Cholesterol

83

Parsley Pesto

Preparation time: 5 minutes

When fresh basil isn't available, or when you want a
change of pace in pesto, try Parsley Pesto. It is wonderful
stirred into a soup, tossed with pasta, or mixed in with
sautéed vegetables.

3 cups packed fresh parsley
$^1/_2$ cup pine nuts
3 cloves garlic, minced
$^1/_8$ teaspoon salt
$^3/_4$ cup olive oil

Place all ingredients in a blender or processor and puree.
When ready to serve, do not heat, simply stir in 1 to 2
tablespoons of water from the pasta to warm pesto before
tossing with noodles or vegetables.

Makes about 2$^1/_2$ cups

Each 2 tablespoon serving provides:

95	Calories	1 g	Carbohydrate
1 g	Protein	5 mg	Sodium
10 g	Fat	0 mg	Cholesterol

84

Mint Fish Sauce

Preparation time: 10 minutes

Mint and fish are an unusual combination, but this works well, especially on broiled fish.

1 cup mint leaves, finely chopped
$^1/_2$ cup parsley leaves, finely chopped
2 tablespoons capers, drained
1 teaspoon sugar
1 egg yolk
1 tablespoon lemon juice
1 teaspoon lemon zest
$^1/_2$ cup olive oil
2 tablespoons fish stock (optional)

Place all ingredients except oil in a blender and puree. Add the oil in a slow stream.

Makes about 1$^1/_2$ cups

	Each 2 tablespoon serving provides:		
91	Calories	2 g	Carbohydrate
0 g	Protein	34 mg	Sodium
10 g	Fat	16 mg	Cholesterol

85

Hungarian Goulash

Preparation time: 90 minutes

This is comfort food for my sons. They look forward to this intense paprika sauce over noodles on those cold and rainy Oregon nights.

1 pound lean round steak, cut into cubes
$^1/_3$ cup extra-virgin olive oil
1 onion, chopped
$^1/_2$ green bell pepper, chopped
1 cup tomato juice
$1^1/_2$ teaspoons paprika
$^1/_4$ teaspoon pepper

In a large, heavy pot, heat oil and sauté meat about 20 minutes. Add onion and bell pepper and cook until soft. Add tomato juice, paprika, and pepper, cover, and simmer for an hour or more. Add additional tomato juice or water if needed. Ladle over cooked wide noodles or potatoes.

Makes about 4 cups

Each $^1/_2$ cup serving provides:

203	Calories	4 g	Carbohydrate
17 g	Protein	151 mg	Sodium
13 g	Fat	44 mg	Cholesterol

86

Garlic-Walnut Sauce

Preparation time: 10 minutes (plus 1 hour standing time)

This recipe has eastern European roots, where it is used on chicken, pork, and vegetables.

2 cups walnuts, chopped
5 cloves garlic, minced
½ cup parsley, chopped
1 cup low-salt chicken broth
4 tablespoons fresh lemon juice
¼ teaspoon turmeric
¼ teaspoon ground coriander
Pinch of cayenne
¼ teaspoon salt
2 tablespoons cilantro, chopped

Combine walnuts, garlic, and parsley in a food processor or blender. Transfer to a bowl and stir in remaining ingredients. Let stand at room temperature at least 1 hour before serving.

Makes about 3 cups

Each 2 tablespoon serving provides:

67	Calories	2 g	Carbohydrate
2 g	Protein	38 mg	Sodium
6 g	Fat	0 mg	Cholesterol

87

Blended Herb Sauce

Preparation time: 15 minutes

This calls for a lot of herbs and fresh are recommended. If you don't have fresh herbs on hand, use dried but use half of what is called for. It goes with plain meat dishes and fish, but is best with vegetables.

2 tablespoons extra-virgin olive oil
1 shallot, minced
4 teaspoons celery, minced
$\frac{1}{2}$ teaspoon each parsley, chervil, marjoram, sage,
    minced
2 tablespoons white wine vinegar
$\frac{1}{8}$ teaspoon salt
$\frac{1}{8}$ teaspoon pepper

Sauté shallot and celery in oil for 3 to 4 minutes, then add the herbs. Stir well, add vinegar and simmer 10 minutes. Add salt and pepper.

Makes about $\frac{1}{4}$ cup

Each tablespoon serving provides:

65	Calories	1 g	Carbohydrate
0 g	Protein	69 mg	Sodium
7 g	Fat	0 mg	Cholesterol

88

Winter Sauce

Preparation time: 35 minutes

This hearty sauce is good with pork or beef, to mix into stews, pour over potatoes, or incorporate into hamburgers. It can also be used as a cooking sauce for chicken or meatballs.

2 tablespoons olive oil
1 onion, minced
1 stalk celery, finely chopped
1 leek (white part), finely chopped
3 cloves garlic, minced
1 bell pepper, minced
1 teaspoon flour
1 cup chicken or beef broth
$1/2$ cup plum tomatoes, peeled, seeded, and chopped
1 tablespoon tomato paste
3 tablespoons white wine vinegar
$1^{1}/_{2}$ teaspoons paprika
$1/2$ teaspoon marjoram
Pinch of sugar

Sauté onion in oil until soft. Add celery, leek, garlic, and bell pepper and sauté until soft, about 8 minutes. Add flour and stir, then add remaining ingredients and simmer, covered, for 20 minutes.

Makes about 4 cups

Each ½ cup serving provides:

57	Calories	5 g	Carbohydrate
1 g	Protein	118 mg	Sodium
4 g	Fat	0 mg	Cholesterol

89

Quick Barbecue Sauce

Preparation time: 15 minutes

Although I have a general theory that barbecue sauce should be different each time since it's so much fun to experiment, I do rely on this fast, delicious barbecue sauce which will always please.

1 tablespoon vegetable oil
1 small onion, chopped
1 cup water
1 cup ketchup
1 tablespoon Dijon mustard
2 cloves garlic, minced
3 tablespoons wine vinegar
4 tablespoons brown sugar
2 tablespoons Worcestershire sauce
1 teaspoon fresh ginger, grated
Dash of cayenne
1 cup pineapple juice (optional)

Sauté onion in oil until soft. Put all other ingredients in a blender and puree. Now stir in the sautéed onion.

Makes about 3¹/₂ cups

Each ¹/₂ cup serving provides:			
100	Calories	20 g	Carbohydrate
1 g	Protein	509 mg	Sodium
2 g	Fat	0 mg	Cholesterol

90

Summer Fruit Salsa

Preparation time: 15 minutes (plus 10 minutes standing time)

Here is a summer barbecue salsa unusual enough to wake up the most barbecue-jaded palate. Try it with any barbecued meat, especially fish or chicken.

1 pint strawberries, quartered
1 papaya, peeled, seeded, and diced
1 mango, peeled and diced
1 tablespoon lime juice
1 tablespoon sugar
1/2 serrano pepper, seeded and minced
1 tablespoon epazote (or mint), minced

Combine all ingredients in a bowl and stir. Let stand 10 minutes.

Makes about 2 cups

Each 1/4 cup serving provides:

52	Calories	13 g	Carbohydrate
1 g	Protein	3 mg	Sodium
0 g	Fat	0 mg	Cholesterol

91

Lemon Mustard Tarragon Marinade

Preparation time: 10 minutes (plus 1 hour marinating time)

The slightly licorice-like flavor of the tarragon combines nicely with the mustard and chives for a tangy fish marinade. Use it for grilled halibut.

¹/₂ cup fresh lemon juice
1 tablespoon lemon zest
¹/₃ cup Dijon mustard
3 to 4 tablespoons fresh tarragon, chopped
2 tablespoons chives or scallions, chopped
¹/₄ cup extra-virgin olive oil
¹/₄ teaspoon black pepper, freshly ground

Combine lemon juice and zest, mustard, tarragon, and chives. Slowly whisk in olive oil then stir in pepper. Pour marinade over the fish, coating all. Marinate 1 hour.

Makes about 1¹/₄ cups, enough for 5 to 6 fish fillets

Each ¹/₄ cup serving provides:

132	Calories	4 g	Carbohydrate
1 g	Protein	428 mg	Sodium
13 g	Fat	0 mg	Cholesterol

92

Garlic-Paprika Sauce

Preparation time: 10 minutes

This very tangy sauce is terrific with grilled meats, especially pork. It can either be spread on the meat before grilling or served on the side.

6 cloves garlic, minced
$^{1}/_{2}$ teaspoon paprika
$^{1}/_{4}$ teaspoon salt
$^{1}/_{8}$ cup extra-virgin olive oil
$^{1}/_{4}$ teaspoon fresh sage, minced

In a mortar, crush the garlic, paprika, and salt until smooth. Add olive oil and blend, then stir in the sage.

Makes about $^{1}/_{4}$ cup

Each tablespoon serving provides:

61	Calories	0 g	Carbohydrate
0 g	Protein	133 mg	Sodium
7 g	Fat	0 mg	Cholesterol

93

Sweet Chile Sauce

Preparation time: 2 hours

This sauce works best as a base for cooking sausage and other meats, and is especially tangy with beans. Bake the meat or beans in the prepared sauce, pour on top, or serve as you would a relish on the side. This has a nice, sweet, barbecue-sauce-like flavor.

4 tomatoes, sliced and seeded
$1/2$ cup tomato juice
$1/2$ cup water
2 bell peppers, 1 red and 1 green, chopped
1 stalk celery, sliced
1 red onion, chopped
1 tablespoon lemon juice
1 teaspoon salt
1 cup light-brown sugar
1 tablespoon cinnamon
$1/2$ cup cider vinegar
$1/8$ teaspoon ground cloves
1 teaspoon prepared mustard

Put tomatoes, tomato juice, water, peppers, celery, onion, lemon juice, salt, and sugar into a large saucepan. Bring to a boil, stirring to dissolve the sugar. Gently simmer for 30 minutes uncovered, stirring occasionally. Add remaining ingredients and cook for an hour, stirring occasionally. Add water if needed.

Makes about 4 cups

Each ½ cup serving provides:

144	Calories	36 g	Carbohydrate
1 g	Protein	348 mg	Sodium
0 g	Fat	0 mg	Cholesterol

94

Andrew's Sweet & Sour BBQ Sauce

Preparation time: 20 minutes

My son Andrew loves sweet and sour Chinese, so this barbecue sauce was created especially for him. Use on hamburgers, ribs, or any barbecue fare.

1 to 2 teaspoons vegetable oil
1 small onion, minced
1/4 teaspoon fresh ginger, grated
1 clove garlic, minced
1 cup ketchup
2 tablespoons tomato paste
1/4 cup brown sugar
2 tablespoons molasses
1/4 cup cider vinegar
1/4 cup Worcestershire sauce
1 tablespoon prepared mustard
Pinch of cayenne
1/2 cup pineapple, chopped

Sauté onion, ginger, and garlic in oil for 5 minutes. Remove from heat and let cool, then place in a bowl with the remaining ingredients, except the pineapple. Whisk together well, then stir in pineapple.

Makes about 3 cups

Each 1/2 cup serving provides:

141	Calories	33 g	Carbohydrate
1 g	Protein	636 mg	Sodium
1 g	Fat	0 mg	Cholesterol

95

Asian Barbecue Sauce

Preparation time: 1 hour 15 minutes

An unusual East meets West mixture, I use it as I do any other barbecue sauce.

2 onions, minced
1 to 2 tablespoons vegetable oil
1 28-ounce can tomatoes
1 cup rice vinegar
2 tablespoons brown sugar
1 teaspoon salt
2 teaspoons fresh ginger, grated
1 teaspoon pepper
1 tablespoon sesame oil
$^{1}/_{8}$ cup soy sauce
2 tablespoons molasses
$^{1}/_{4}$ cup orange juice
$^{1}/_{8}$ cup Dijon mustard

Sauté onions in oil until soft, about 5 minutes. Add remaining ingredients, slicing the tomatoes in half in the pan, and simmer for 1 hour, stirring occasionally. Place in a blender and puree.

Makes about 3 $^{1}/_{2}$ cups

Each $^{1}/_{2}$ cup serving provides:

116	Calories	18 g	Carbohydrate
2 g	Protein	899 mg	Sodium
5 g	Fat	0 mg	Cholesterol

96

Rosemary-Garlic Marinade

Preparation time: 10 minutes (plus 30 minutes marinating time)

I had to include this fabulous marinade, my summer favorite. It is perfect for grilled chicken.

4 cloves garlic, minced
3 tablespoons extra-virgin olive oil
2 tablespoons fresh rosemary, chopped
2 teaspoons fresh lemon juice
1/8 teaspoon salt
1/8 teaspoon pepper

Combine all ingredients and brush over chicken, covering well. Marinate 30 minutes.

Makes enough to coat 2 chicken breasts or 1 whole chicken

Each 2 tablespoon serving provides:

97	Calories	2 g	Carbohydrate
0 g	Protein	68 mg	Sodium
10 g	Fat	0 mg	Cholesterol

97

Pear Sauce

Preparation time: 20 minutes (plus time to cool)

Serve this pear sauce as you would applesauce, with pork, or on its own. It's also great atop fresh berries or pancakes.

2 pears, peeled, cored, and sliced
3 tablespoons lemon juice
1/2 cup sugar
1 tablespoon cornstarch
1 cup water

Process the pears and lemon juice in a blender until smooth, then pour into a saucepan. Add remaining ingredients and bring to a boil. Reduce heat and simmer, stirring constantly for 1 minute. Remove from heat and cool before serving.

Makes about 2 cups

Each 1/2 cup serving provides:

149	Calories	39 g	Carbohydrate
0 g	Protein	2 mg	Sodium
0 g	Fat	0 mg	Cholesterol

98

Mango Sauce

Preparation time: 10 minutes (plus time to chill)

A plain dessert can become something exotic with this tropical sauce. It's good on cakes or with ice cream, or dip shortbread cookies in it.

2 ripe mangoes, peeled, pitted, and chopped
1 tablespoon fresh orange juice
1 tablespoon fresh lemon juice
1 tablespoon honey

Place all in a blender and process until smooth. Strain the sauce into a bowl, then chill.

Makes about 1¹/₂ cups

Each 2 tablespoon serving provides:

29	Calories	8 g	Carbohydrate
0 g	Protein	1 mg	Sodium
0 g	Fat	0 mg	Cholesterol

99

Fresh Fruit Sauce

Preparation time: 15 minutes

Fresh Fruit Sauce is for desserts, for melons, or to use as a dipping sauce with cookies. With this basic recipe you can make many fruits into a quick sauce. This works especially well with raspberries and strawberries. If using peaches or plums, peel and seed.

$^{1}/_{4}$ cup sugar
$^{1}/_{4}$ cup water
$^{1}/_{4}$ cup orange juice
2 tablespoons cornstarch
$2^{1}/_{4}$ cups fresh fruit, chopped

Bring sugar, water, orange juice, and cornstarch to a boil. Add about $1^{1}/_{2}$ cups of the fruit, then return to a boil. Remove from heat and add remaining fruit. Stir, but do not cook.

Makes about 2 cups

Each $^{1}/_{4}$ cup serving provides:

46	Calories	12 g	Carbohydrate
0 g	Protein	1 mg	Sodium
0 g	Fat	0 mg	Cholesterol

100

Yogurt-Orange Syrup

Preparation time: 5 minutes (plus time to chill)

Here's a simple and quick treat for crepes or pancakes.

1 cup nonfat or lowfat yogurt
½ cup fresh orange juice
2 tablespoons maple syrup

Mix together and serve chilled or at room temperature.

Makes about 1½ cups

Each 2 tablespoon serving provides:

23	Calories	5 g	Carbohydrate
1 g	Protein	14 mg	Sodium
0 g	Fat	0 mg	Cholesterol

101

Maple-Hazelnut Sauce

Preparation time: 15 minutes

Delightful on pancakes, great on desserts, the blend of hazlenuts and maple is a natural.

$^3/_4$ cup hazelnuts toasted and finely chopped
2 cups maple syrup
$^1/_8$ cup fresh orange juice, strained
Dash of cinnamon
Dash of nutmeg

Combine nuts, maple syrup, and orange juice in a saucepan and simmer 10 minutes. Add cinnamon and nutmeg and stir briefly.

Makes about 2$^3/_4$ cups

Each $^1/_4$ cup serving provides:

205	Calories	38 g	Carbohydrate
1 g	Protein	6 mg	Sodium
7 g	Fat	0 mg	Cholesterol

Index